PLANET
PROTECTORS!

May you have lots of fun
being planet protectors!
Ruth

D0415864

52 WAYS TO LOOK AFTER GOD'S WORLD

PLANET PROTECTORS!

spck

PAUL KERENSA & RUTH VALERIO

illustrated by Fay Austin

To our own Planet Protectors:
Joseph and Phoebe,
Mali and Jemba.

Thank you for keeping us on our toes
and being an inspiration.

———

First published in Great Britain in 2021

Society for Promoting Christian Knowledge
36 Causton Street
London SW1P 4ST
www.spck.org.uk

British Library Cataloguing-in-Publication Data
A catalogue record for this book is available from the British Library

ISBN 978–0–281–08545–3

1 3 5 7 9 10 8 6 4 2

First printed by Imago

Subsequently digitally printed in Great Britain

This book is 100% recyclable. It is produced on paper from sustainable forests
and printed with environmentally friendly inks

CONTENTS

INTRODUCTION

Hello! I'm Ruth. I love helping people to look after this amazing world. I've discovered that doing so can be a fun adventure, so I'm excited to help **you** think about what you can do too as you read this book.

And I'm Paul. I love this planet. In fact, I think I'll stay here, but I'm trying to get better at taking care of it! There are things we've started doing as a family that I think all add up to a **BIG** difference for this lovely world we call home.

We're so pleased you're going to read this book. Looking after the world God has made is an awesome thing to do and, let's face it, the grown-ups have messed it up. So you're being given a challenge: will **you** be a Planet Protector?

It doesn't matter if you've never really thought about looking after the planet till now – or if you've been doing it for years. Whoever you are, it's what you do now that matters! Reckon you can do it? We reckon you can!

This book is all about how to be a brilliant Planet Protector. It's got lots of information and lots of ideas for things you can do – on your own, at school, with your family and with your church.

You can work your way through the book or open it on any page you like.

Maybe go through it with your family?

> Oh, and those gaps on pages? They're for you to fill in! Go for it. This is *your* book. Write down how you're getting on. You can encourage yourself by seeing how well you're doing.

HAPPY READING – AND THEN...HAPPY DOING!

#1 GOING BANANAS

Do you like bananas? They're the world's most popular fruit! (All right, tomatoes **MIGHT** be more popular – but are tomatoes really a fruit? You wouldn't put one in a fruit salad.)

We go bananas for bananas. So supermarkets try to keep them cheap. A banana used to cost 18p. Now you can buy them for 11p each! Most things go up in price over time. Bananas are going down! That's bananas.

18p – 11p = 7p. So who's losing out on that 7p? Farmers and field workers. They need that money. 100 billion x 7p = **A LOT!**

Some supermarkets thought that they'd be **SUPER** supermarkets and agreed to buy and sell **Fairtrade** bananas. That means they pay farmers a fixed price for those tasty bananas (plus a little extra on top) – so the farmers won't lose money.

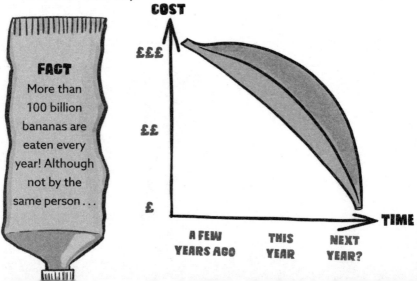

FACT
More than 100 billion bananas are eaten every year! Although not by the same person . . .

COST

£££

££

£

TIME

A FEW YEARS AGO

THIS YEAR

NEXT YEAR?

If God wants fairness in our world, shouldn't we try to be fair to everyone? Sounds fair, right?

But some supermarkets **DON'T** sell Fairtrade things. If it's not Fairtrade, it might be **UN**fair trade! Especially if it's super-cheap – the people who got that banana to your fruit bowl might not be paid enough to live on.

NEXT STEPS

- If you see Fairtrade bananas or chocolate for sale, buy them rather than the non-Fairtrade ones. They might cost a little more, but that money's going to the farmers.

- If your supermarket doesn't sell Fairtrade bananas, email or write to them! Get a reply? Put it in this page to remind you that you can make a difference.

- Does your church or school buy fruit sometimes? Is *THAT* Fairtrade? Why not ask whoever's in charge? It might make them think.

FILL IN HERE

What Fairtrade items can you find in your local supermarket?

Look for bananas, chocolate, tea and coffee. List any you find here.

....

....

....

....

....

....

....

....

....

....

....

....

....

See a Fairtrade item in the shops? Buy it, keep the label, stick it on this page!

See how many you can collect!

#2 HOW FAR I'LL GO

Do you recognize this title? It's a song from the film *Moana*. She's looking at the water, wondering how far she'll go in life, but first...she sings! She's stuck on an island, so she's stuck with walking if it's near or sailing if it's far. But how far is far for you?

Is your school too far to walk to? How about where your friends live? The park? The shops?

FILL IN HERE

How would you normally get around locally? Walk? Cycle? Drive? Bus? Train?

Boat, maybe, if you live on an island, like Moana!

I would...to get to school.

We'd get to the shops by..

I'd...................................to get to my friend's house.

For the nearest park, I'd..

I'd...to go on holiday.

In our daily lives, do we sometimes do what's *convenient* instead of what's best?

Hmm. 'What's best.' What's best for who? Me and my feet? My busy day? God's planet?

Each time we drive short distances, we're putting polluting things into the air around us, from our car's fumes. Petrol and diesel cars release poisonous gases – pretty much the worst is a nasty whiff called **carbon monoxide**.

FACT

Did you know that 80 per cent of lung problems are because of car pollution? Oh, and vans. And lorries... But not bikes!

When we walk or cycle, we do very little to the air around us (depending on what we've eaten...). Walking and cycling short distances can be a small start to making a **BIG** difference. Because every journey adds up!

Look at that list you wrote. Are there any travel methods you could change?

I always thought that school was too far to walk to, but I've had an idea...

No, I'm not giving you a piggyback ride!

WHAT CAN I DO?

- Think about what a 'short distance' is. As we grow, does what we think of as a short distance change too?

- Come back to this page in a week or more. Can you change any of the words you've written above to 'walking' or 'cycling'? Maybe how you get about can change...

- Next time you walk or cycle, think about three things on that trip that you wouldn't have seen or felt if you'd been in a car instead. Put them here if you like.

Three things I spotted on today's walk/cycle (that I wouldn't have spotted in a car):

....

....

....

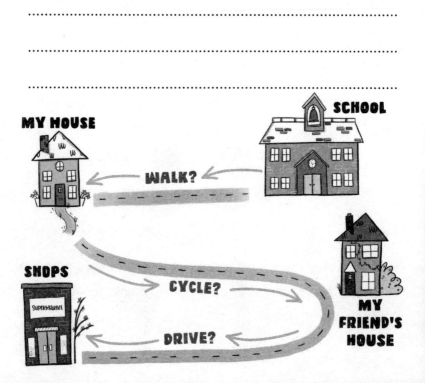

3 ▸ DEAR MP...OR PM...

Who's your MP (that's your Member of Parliament – the person who should represent your views to government)? If you live in the UK, you'll have one. MPs take issues that local people care about and can bring them to Parliament.

Find out your MP's name and write it here...........................

....

You can also find out his or her address or email address at this website: <https://members.parliament.uk>. Write it here...

....

....

....

Then write it on an envelope. Or ask an adult to help start an email to your MP.

Yes, you can write to your MP! Perhaps let her or him know what changes you'd like to see locally (does your park welcome wildlife – or litter?) or nationally (is there a campaign you want to shout about?)

Have a practice on the next page. **BUT** write it out again to send properly!

Today's date:..................

Dear .... (*Your MP's name here – be polite!*)

(*Introduce yourself. How old are you? Where do you go to school? MPs like it when you're local!*) ....
....

(*Get your MP's attention with a fact or short statement saying what you're writing about – keep on topic!*)...............................
....
....
....

(*Do you have a solution in mind? What are you asking for? What can you suggest as the best thing to do?*) ....
....
....
....

(*What do you want to happen now? Could you invite your MP to speak to your school? Raise an issue in Parliament? Support a campaign?*) ....
....

(*If you'd like a reply, ask for one!*) ....
....

(*Politely say goodbye and sign your name*) ....
....

Hey, one day, maybe you could be an MP and get letters like this sent to you!

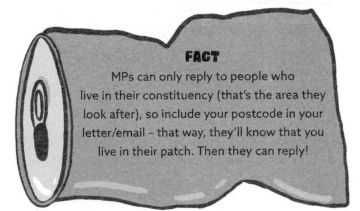

FACT
MPs can only reply to people who live in their constituency (that's the area they look after), so include your postcode in your letter/email – that way, they'll know that you live in their patch. Then they can reply!

Can you help me with some of the big words?

Of course I can. Don't write them so big next time!

#4 LOVE YOUR COAT!

Do you have a coat? Yes, but is it a GOOD coat? Is it the sort of coat that's actually a bit leaky and has never been quite the same since that blizzard last year? Or are you lucky and it's the sort of coat that you can boldly wear and go out in any weather – shower or storm, drizzle or downpour? I mean a nice waterproof, ready for adventure and excitement!

Oh, and while you're there, does everyone in your family have a good coat? Is anyone ready for a new one?

A few years ago, I had a coat. It wasn't a good coat. Every time it rained, I put off wearing my coat – it was a bit small and the water seeped through. Then, for my birthday, someone bought me a coat. A proper waterproof that's big enough and warm enough and dry enough! I've spent longer in the garden and on walks ever since.

Learning to love your coat means...

• Just because it's raining, we don't always drive to places we could walk to. So what, if it's a rainy walk to school!

- We spend longer in the garden or other local outside places – whatever the weather.

- We can plant, climb, step over, dig up, count crawling things, bird-watch, litter-pick, explore God's world, tend God's world...

The list is endless!

Add your ideas here

....

....

....

Oh, and learn to love boots too. And jumpers, if it's cold. And cups of hot drink when we come in.

#5 BEACHCOMBING

There's a psalm – an old song – in the Bible:

Let's sing for joy to the Lord...
Let's come before him with thanksgiving...music and song.
The sea is his, for he made it,
and his hands formed the dry land.

(Our take on Psalm 95)

If God made the sea, and if his hands formed the dry land, then he'll want us to look after those places, right? If I made something, I wouldn't want it covered in things that are not meant to be there.

So, find the right day – it doesn't have to be the nicest weather, just a day when the family's free – and **GET TO THE BEACH!** All right, if the beach is a long way away, is there a lake or river nearby instead?

It's not a sunbathing day, though. Oh no. It's something much more satisfying. **A BIG CLEAN!**

Where the land meets the sea, all sorts of things wash up on the beach.

FACT
Every day, 8 million pieces of plastic find their way into our sea. Into God's sea! They not only make a mess, they also kill the creatures that live in the sea. That's terrible!

Plastic bottles, plastic bags...They might have been washed out to sea and washed in again. How much can you collect? Pick up what you can (be safe if there are sharp bits!) and take it all to a recycling bin or centre. Then know that you've helped clean what God's made, what he's formed with his hands.

Like the psalm, maybe we can sing as we go!

Pick pick pick pick litter, pick a little litter for me...

What did you find on the beach? Where do you think it started life? Where do you think it will end up now?

I found...	Maybe it started life... (*use your imagination!*)	It'll end up...
A plastic bottle	In a beachfront café in Spain?	In my local recycling centre. It might become another bottle!
....	....	....
....	....	....
....	....	....
....	....	....
....	....	....

REAL-LIFE PLANET PROTECTORS!

Meet Holly and Isla (7)

We are identical twins, Holly and Isla, and we're seven years old. We've been learning at school since Reception about climate change and how important it is to protect and help save our planet.

We both love to swim and the beach is our favourite place to be. In fact, our mum is helping us write this while we're on a beach holiday in Cornwall. It makes us very sad seeing litter everywhere and when we see people leaving rubbish, especially single-use plastic waste that is harmful to the animals and the ocean.

We pick up litter along the way when we're out and about for walks. We have also inspired our mum to open a zero-waste shop where we live and we think every place should have one![1]

A zero-waste shop is where you can come to reuse your existing containers and refill them with dried cupboard essentials, such as rice and pasta, and household cleaning essentials, such as washing-up liquid and hand soap. These are eco-friendly products that are not harmful to the planet *and* it helps to reduce plastic waste at the same time.

We may be little, but we care about our planet very much. We believe that if we all make small changes at home by rethinking, reusing, repurposing and refilling before recycling, then we can all do our part to help save our planet.

[1] Have a look at <https://twinlarder.co.uk>.

#6   THE BIG SORT

There's nothing like a really good sort-out . . . moving on those toys and clothes you've outgrown. They've brought you joy and fun – now let them bring happiness to someone else!

Donating to charity shops – and buying from them, too – is a great way to make sure that we waste less. Do you really need that plastic toy to be new?

Plan an afternoon, tell your family – maybe they can join in too. Time to move on that green and orange shirt that, come on, should never have come into the house to begin with . . .

Remember: charity shops want nice things. These are for other people to buy and use, so we should always look after our things and then donate them to a charity shop or give them to friends who could use them, maybe with kids younger than us.

What items have you found in your sorting? What could happen to them next?

This was mine...	Next it could go to...
A stripy jumper	My neighbour who likes warm 'n' funky clothes!
....	....
....	....
....	....
....	....

What about donations that shops don't want? Some are sold overseas, often to African countries such as Kenya, Ghana and the Ivory Coast. Good-quality clothes might be sold at a fair price, looking after African workers. If we send bad old clothes overseas, though, it can harm local clothes businesses because it leaves them with piles of clothes that they don't know what to do with, while also stopping them selling the clothes that they make themselves!

Hmm... So what should we do, then?

It's still good to donate, but it's even better to... BUY from a charity shop!

So...

- Good-quality clothes can go to a charity shop.

- Not-so-good-quality clothes (or towels and sheets) can go to be recycled in a clothing/textiles bank (these might be in your supermarket car park).

- *No material should ever be thrown away!*

It takes a lot of energy to make clothes, so let's use them.

If we buy second hand (and look after our clothes and toys), we treasure what we have...and we don't swamp other countries with our own unwanted clothes!

FILL IN HERE

Chat to the rest of your family about where they get their clothes from – and what they do with them after they've finished with them.

....

....

....

....

....

....

BIN BATTLE

Where's your bin?

No, where's your WHEELIE-bin?

I bin in the garden.

I weally bin in the garden!

In the next few weeks, you're going to have a bin battle. (Don't worry – it won't get messy.) You're going to do battle with that most equal of foes . . . yourself.

As a house, how many bin bags do you think you get through each week?

Put your guess here: ....

I'm sure that you recycle when you can – you're a Planet Protector – but there are always things that end up in the big grey bin (other colours are available), things we call **REFUSE**.

But what if you refuse to use **REFUSE?** Can you improve on your bin bag total?

Make a chart to put near the door where you take the bins out. Ask your family to put a '1' on the chart every time they put a bin bag out or they can tell you and you can fill it in!

BIN BAG TOT-UP

Week 1: ....

Week 2: ....

Week 3: ....

You can keep counting after Week 3 if you like.

Can you improve each week? What do you throw away lots of? What can you do to change that?

We'll always throw away some things, but let's challenge ourselves to throw away as little as possible. That way, we're respecting God's planet by not filling up landfill sites.

HERE'S AN EXTRA THOUGHT...

TWO BILLION people on the planet don't have their rubbish collected. Visit <www.bintwinning.org> to see what you can do to help. Pay to 'twin your bin' and you'll get a certificate and a photo of the rubbish collection that YOU have helped to pay for. It keeps people healthy and hygienic – and keeps their streets clean.

BEE FRIENDLY

In the Bible (Genesis 2, if you want to know) it says, right at the start, that God put the person in the garden to work it and take care of it.

That means we've all been made to be gardeners and to look after the land around us!

I wonder . . . does your school have an allotment? A vegetable patch? A science garden? Anywhere you can **GROW** things? Maybe your house does? Your church?! ('Dear church leader. . . Would you consider having a church allotment . . . ?')

We know it's good to be friendly. Did you also know it's good to be bee-friendly? And butterfly-friendly? We need bees and butterflies because they pollinate plants and so enable food to grow. Without them (and wasps and hoverflies) we wouldn't be able to grow food or have so many different sorts of food. They're beautiful too, and our gardens would be boring without them!

Oh dear. My garden is mostly paving slabs, but I'll plant and grow what I can, where I can!

Window boxes, plants in pots, flowers in borders and containers . . . We can do LOADS to encourage nice, flying, buzzy things.

Ask at your local garden centre or search for 'bee-friendly plants' on <www.ecosia.org>. (Heard of Google? Ecosia does a very similar thing – searches the Internet for you – except it plants trees. It plants more trees the more people search. Wow!)

BEE A PAL

Which bee is buzzing to which flower?

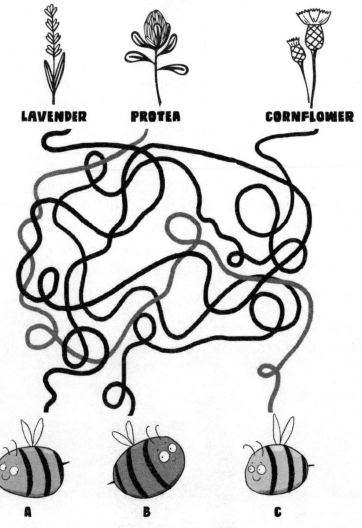

LAVENDER   PROTEA   CORNFLOWER

A   B   C

VEG, VEG, VEG

In the very first chapter of the Bible, God says, 'Look! I have given you every seed-bearing plant throughout the earth and all the fruit trees for your food.' It's God's way of saying . . . **'EAT YOUR GREENS!'**

Well, they are tasty.

Meat-eating comes later in the Bible, but back in the Garden of Eden, in the perfect picture the Bible paints for us . . . eating veg is best.

It's good for us, and it's good for the planet. Meat production needs **A LOT** of energy. Can you believe that you need about **8 kilos of grain** and – wait for it – about **15,415 litres of water** to produce **just 1 kilo of beef!**

So . . .

- If you eat meat, try eating less of it. Could you start by having one or two (or five or six . . .) meals a week that don't have meat in them?

- If you eat meat, buy it from people who look after their animals. Free-range, well-kept . . . Looking after animals is part of our God-given job!

- Talk to your church about going #defaultveg for any meals provided there.

'Default' means the thing we do automatically. So #defaultveg is a campaign to only add meat if people ask for it.
Ah, so my room is default untidy? Got it.

	Vegetable	How much I like it
		(marks out of 10)
An orange vegetable	....	....
A vegetable that grows in the ground	....	....
A vegetable that looks like a small tree	....	....
A vegetable that begins with 'P'	....	....
A vegetable high in protein (check any packets in your kitchen)	....	....
A vegetable that can be red	....	....
A vegetable the size of your head!	....	....
A vegetable so small that you'd need 100 to fill you up	....	....
A vegetable that – sniff – can make you cry	....	....
A vegetable that you might eat for your Christmas dinner	....	....
A vegetable often found in tins	....	....
A vegetable with layers	....	....
The tastiest vegetable!	....	....

WELCOME!

Did you know that 1 in every 110 people in the world is a refugee or asylum seeker or unable to go back home? You might have a family in your street, in your school or in your church just like this. Jesus' family were refugees. So was Abraham. The Bible is FULL of refugees and today's world is too.

Do you make them feel extra welcome?

The Bible says, 'Don't look out only for your own interests, but take an interest in others too' (Philippians 2.4). If we're going to be Planet Protectors, that means protecting the people who share the planet with us as well.

There's a new boy in my class who speaks Arabic. I've not said hello to him yet.

You could say welcome. Try **ahlan wa sahlaan**. That means 'welcome' in Arabic!

REFUGEE REASONS

People don't choose to become refugees. So why does it happen?

Sometimes it's to escape violence. Perhaps their country is at war and it's unsafe – or they may no longer have a home there. Sometimes climate change has meant that whole communities have to move. For some people, it's because of their beliefs – they could be Christian, Muslim or any other religion and find that they're not welcome where they live.

NEXT STEPS

If a refugee child came to your school, how could you make him or her feel welcome?

(Help with school equipment? School welcome pack? Invitation to an event?)

....

....

Many refugees are in refugee camps across the world – homeless and unsure where to go next. What could you do for them?

(Pray for them? Write letters to them? Find out more about life in a refugee camp?)

....

....

NO THROW

Ever since God made humans, he made fuel to keep us going. Food, glorious food! We love it, but we love it a bit too much...

In the UK, a THIRD of food gets chucked away. It doesn't even reach a mouth (apart from the mouth of a bin). To put it another way, that's equivalent to...

- **4.5 MILLION tonnes – that's the weight of 1 million elephants!**

- **10 BILLION meals, enough to feed everyone called Dave in America for a year. (I don't know why you'd want to. Are you having a Dave party?)**

The good news? We're getting better. We're throwing away a little less than we used to. The bad news? We're still binning **ALL THAT FOOD!** The carbon footprint is **HUGE** and pointless. All that food waste fuels climate change, which makes life harder for people living in poverty across the world. In a world where so many go hungry, it can't be right to waste so much food.

So let's stop.

WHAT CAN I DO?

The first step is to be more involved in your house food. That means The Shopping and The Cooking.

Think of these three things when you think about food.

- What if we only bought what we needed? Can you plan your meals better? Maybe on a whiteboard or a weekly food planner?

- Have a weekly 'leftovers day', when you make your meals from anything in the fridge that needs to be eaten up. Get creative – what meals could you concoct?!

- Don't forget: 'Best before' dates are different from 'Use by'. Food might be at its BEST BEFORE a certain date...but you can still USE it BY a later date! (Although, if your tub of cream smells of old socks, next time eat it sooner or don't buy so much!)

PLUS TRY THESE GREAT IDEAS TO REUSE FOOD!

What?	What to do with it?	How'd it taste?
Brown bananas	Banana bread/ pancakes/cake!	
Yesterday's veggies	Today's soup!	
Old salad	Cook it up!	
Stale bread	Breadcrumb topping on dinner!	

BE VOCAL ABOUT LOCAL

Would you put a strawberry in a seat on an aeroplane?

Check in some asparagus for a flight from Peru to Manchester?

Offer an in-flight meal to a family of green beans? ('We are happy to serve you . . . Oh dear, we are actually serving . . . you!')

Probably not, yet these three foodstuffs are some of the most well-travelled in the world! You might not have flown overseas for a while, but you're eating overseas A LOT.

In the Garden of Eden, God gives us food. It's right there at the start (well, we'd have got hungry pretty quickly otherwise). So we should enjoy our food, for sure! We should appreciate food as a gift from God, oh yes! But should we see food as just a convenience? Every possible food, there whenever we want? That was never the plan, but we learnt how to fly and we learnt how to fly food.

Some foods just don't grow so easily in certain seasons, so if you want apples in the summer or raspberries in the winter, you might have to fly them in from other countries. They'll also come wrapped in lots of plastic, which we will throw away. So look into where your food has come from and buy local and seasonal instead, as much as you can.

Hmm... I know that flights have a big effect on the environment. How do I stop my food having so many holidays?

We can buy local where we can. We can go even locatler by growing food at home, in the back garden! (And no, 'locatler' isn't a word...)

NEXT STEPS

- You could chat with grown-ups about changing what you – and they – eat.

- Learn online what foods are likely to be grown locally.

MUNCH MAP!

For the next week, on the next page can you label on the map where any of your food has come from? What's travelled furthest? Are there any more local alternatives you could have next time?

This way for an amazing activity!

13 SHOWER POWER

Did you know that:

- **71 per cent of Planet Earth is covered in water (we should really call it Planet Water...)**

- **60 per cent of our own bodies is made of water**

- **60 per cent of the world's population live in places where there's not a sustainable amount of water?**

So if you have water on tap, like, in your tap...you're one of the lucky ones!

I don't like baths or showers.

I know...that is, my nose knows.

The average person uses 980 litres of water A WEEK! That's about seven bathfuls.

Speaking of baths...do you have baths or showers? (Just a flannel to the face when you think about it? You mucky so-and-so!)

Showers use less water than baths (so long as you're not standing there for 20 minutes) and, as you can tell, in this book we don't like waste, so the advice is to shower rather than have a bath.

You could time yourselves too – who has the quickest showers in your house?

You can get a water-saving showerhead that will save EVEN MORE water. Turn off the taps while brushing your teeth too – it all adds up.

Saving water in the UK won't help to save water in far-away countries . . . but by the year 2050, parts of the UK may not have enough water to go around. Unless we use our water better!

Like ALL parts of God's creation, water is a life-giving gift. Let's use it well!

A WEEKLY WATER LOG

Name of person	Number of baths	Number of showers
Dad	1, but he needed it	6
Sister	0	7, including 1 long one (kept singing)
Brother	7	0 – time to start showering?

14 CHILDREN CHANGE CHURCHES, PART 1

Do you go to a church?

Do your church leaders talk about protecting God's planet? Perhaps you could talk to them about it – they might then talk about how we as a Church can do more to look after this lovely world we call home.

There are other ways that you can help your church to take God's world seriously – because your church isn't just a building...it's the people!

So how do you get the people to think more about caring for the world and the issues you care about, from climate change to pollution to endangered species?

Well...have you ever led prayers in church?

It may feel like a scary thing if you've not done it before, but ask your grown-ups to join in if you like. Could you ask to lead prayers as a family one week?

Then make sure that you pray some BIG prayers out loud for the issues you care about. That God helps us care for all of creation. That we all make changes in our own lives for the better. That we think more about the plastic we throw away. That we look after wildlife.

Think about the big green issues you care about most and list them here as prayer points.

....

....

....

....

....

....

....

....

....

Gulp! Can we pray at home quietly instead?

We can, but just think...if we lead prayers in church...God's listening, and others will listen too! They might need to hear what we've got to say.

15 A LOT OF BOTTLE

We've all had days out and needed a drink. It could have been at school or a day out at a zoo or bottle-making factory (unlikely, but you never know).

So what do you drink out of? A bottle!

What sorts of water bottles do you have in your family? Make sure that you each have your own reusable water bottle and make a pact together. Right now. You will never...ever...buy a single-use plastic water bottle again!

Plastic is one of the most brilliant things ever and also one of the worst things we've done to this lovely round home that God's given us. It's EVERYWHERE! We get food and drink packaged in it. Online deliveries often arrive in it. Even our plastic is sometimes delivered in plastic.

PLASTIC-FREE POINTS

Go around your home. Try every room. Give yourself **ONE POINT** for every room with **NO PLASTIC** in it. How many points do you get?

Write it here: ....

Need to work on it? Come back to this page in a few weeks' time and do another count of your plastic-free rooms.

Put your new answer here: ....

Any improvement?!

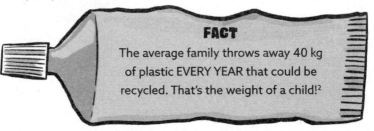

FACT
The average family throws away 40 kg of plastic EVERY YEAR that could be recycled. That's the weight of a child![2]

There's no need to buy a single-use bottle (ugh). Even if you're putting a single-use plastic bottle (ugh) into the recycling, it's still not good for our lovely planet.

Single-*use* becomes ref*use* VERY quickly.

And what's the *use* in that?

[2] Don't throw away plastic or children.
Recycle plastic and keep children just where they are.

16 ENERGY MONITOR

You might find that there are two locked white boxes attached to your home. Some people have them inside their home, but for us they're stuck on the brickwork next to the downstairs loo window. Inside each one is a machine that slowly counts numbers upwards.

These are our gas and electricity meters. One tells the gas company how much gas we're using and the other does the same for electricity. Then they charge us the right amount of money (but they're also great for checking we're not using too much).

Every few months, the gas and electric companies email us asking us to read the meters – to let them know how much energy our home is using. The energy companies used to send people round to check...then they asked us to check it ourselves...and now in our home the children do the checking. They carefully write down the numbers and we let the energy companies know (an adult could double-check – otherwise you might pay the wrong amount for your energy!).

You might have a key meter instead. Keep tabs on how often your grown-ups top it up and see how slowly you can use that energy before it needs to be topped up again.

Checking regularly helps us to think about the gas and electricity we're using all the time. The more energy we use, the more nasty whiffs can go into our atmosphere.

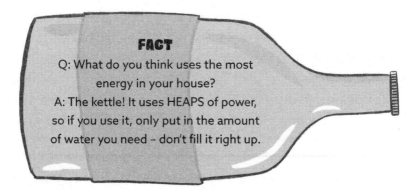

FACT

Q: What do you think uses the most energy in your house?

A: The kettle! It uses HEAPS of power, so if you use it, only put in the amount of water you need – don't fill it right up.

Can you think of ways to reduce the amount of energy used each month?

Some ideas to get you started . . .

Turn lights off when not using them

....

Make sure that your home is properly insulated! Keep the heat in

....

....

....

....

....

....

....

....

....

....

NEXT STEPS

- Chat with your grown-ups about what you've found.

- Chat with them too about switching to a renewable energy supplier – that way, wind, sun, the tides and all sorts of natural things can help to power your TV and games console!

The numbers keep going up every time I check the meters!

Yup! We as the human race just keeeep using energy, but we can try to use less. Before you put the heating on, put on a jumper!

#17 INSIDE OUT

Is the weather nice?

Do you have to be indoors for something?

No, but do you **have** to?

School lessons, family meals, church...Could any of these move outside instead of inside? You'll have to ask whoever's leading or running the thing reeeeeeeeally nicely. He or she might still say no, but...

An inspiring man called Richard Louv has come up with the term 'nature deficit disorder' – the idea that we're spending more and more time inside. It's bad for our health and happiness when we're not outside, experiencing nature.

- **What if your school held a lesson outside?** Science can teach you about nature. In English, you can make up poems about the sun and trees and grass. Geography can get you thinking about the nature you have around you, compared to that around someone in another country, perhaps where there are droughts and rising temperatures.

Let us know when you've tried it! Was it good?

Yes/A bit/Here's what happened

....

....

- **What if you had a family meal outside?** Studies show that we're less stressed when we eat outside. Also, we can get vitamin D from the sun while we're getting other vitamins from our veggies. Plus, eating honey when you can actually hear bees? Nothing like it. (Just don't let them near it.)

Let us know when you've tried it! Was it good?

Yes/A bit/Here's what happened

....

....

- **What if your church met outside on a nice sunny day?** You could appreciate and pray for and apprayciate (great new word) so much more about the outside world than you can from the inside.

Let us know when you've tried it! Was it good?

Yes/A bit/Here's what happened

....

....

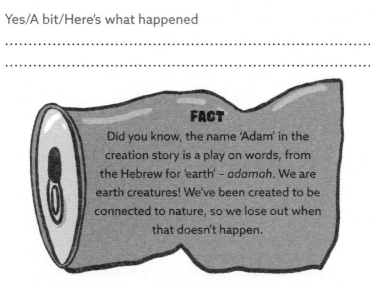

FACT
Did you know, the name 'Adam' in the creation story is a play on words, from the Hebrew for 'earth' – *adamah*. We are earth creatures! We've been created to be connected to nature, so we lose out when that doesn't happen.

#18 FLYING WITHOUT WINGS?

Humans are funny. We don't have wings but we are **ADDICTED** to flying.

From family holidays to grown-ups flying for work meetings (or children flying for work meetings, I guess) – even within this country – it's a habit that we've found tricky to break.

We think flying's normal – after all, everyone seems to do it. We don't think about the harm it does to the environment.

Planes spew out gases – carbon monoxide, carbon dioxide, sulphur oxides, nitrogen oxides, black carbon – as well as various microscopic pieces of matter known as 'particulates' and lead. Then there's the noise pollution of living under flight paths. Flying is a **BIG** cause of climate change and we *have* to change our habits if we're going to have any hope of tackling that.

WHAT CAN I DO?

Look at what flying happens in your family (if any). We've learnt that work meetings can happen virtually. Have fun experimenting with getting places on the train (<www.seat61.com> has some good rail-based travel ideas). Set yourselves some ground(ed) rules: no flying within the UK and Europe. One flying family holiday every other year/every two years/every five years…

There are some **GREAT** places to holiday without flying.

Search on <www.ecosia.com> or look at a map or guidebook and list some places that you'd like to go **in this country**.

....

....

....

....

....

I've had some great holidays overseas. There was a beach with a huge sandcastle and my dad swam in the sea eating an ice-cream! Was that Spain or Greece?

You sent me a postcard. It was Bournemouth. In England!

#19 ▶ FAST FASHION

Fast fashion is not a good thing!

What? Being fast is normally good! Fashion means wearing nice things... doesn't it?

But put them together and it means DISASTER.

It used to be that we had fewer clothes, paid more for them, looked after them and they lasted longer. Then some of the people who sell us clothes had the idea that the more clothes we buy, the more money they get. Fast fashion means cheap clothing that we might wear for a bit, then throw away. Not good for God's planet!

That is because (as we'll see in the next chapter) all those clothes use extraordinary amounts of raw materials, such as cotton, water, pesticides and plastic, and they cause problems as we then fill up our landfill sites with all the clothes we throw away.

It also puts extra pressure on the factory owners and workers to provide clothes as cheaply as possible.

Who are the people making our clothes? They're mostly women in factories **THOUSANDS** of miles away, working very long hours for not much money. Most of the money we pay for our clothes goes to the shop that sells them and the factory owners.

WHAT CAN I DO?

• Buy second hand.

• Buy from ethical clothing companies (search for them on Ecosia).

• Look after your clothes and keep them for longer.

Think about where your clothes have come from. Read the labels in your clothing to see where it was made. 'Made in ...' – where? Can you find the country on a map?

Pray for those who made your clothes.

A PRAYER FOR THE PEOPLE WHO MADE THE CLOTHES I'M WEARING

Write yours here!

....

....

....

.... Amen.

COTTON ON

Just done the previous page? Then, if you've been looking at the labels in your clothes... keep reading!

What are your clothes made from? Does it say on the label – 50 per cent this, 10 per cent that, 40 per cent the other?

Unfortunately, the fashion industry is the third most environmentally damaging industry after oil and meat production. Clothes factories send out **FIVE TIMES** more carbon into the air than all of our planes do!

Cotton is in a lot of our clothing, but there are two types: organic cotton (the better one) and non-organic cotton (the bad one – most clothing is made from this). Non-organic cotton uses lots of water and lots of pesticides are used when growing that cotton. Also, cotton farmers aren't paid very much at all for their crops, so look for Fairtrade cotton when you can.

Other materials are used to make clothes too – but a lot of the time they're 'synthetic'. That means it's a plastic material, which is made from lots of oil and sheds tiny bits of plastic – *microplastics* – into your washing machine when you wash it. Those microplastics end up in our rivers and seas, *and our sea animals don't like that for their breakfast!* As Planet Protectors we can help by following the suggestions for what you can do in the previous chapter. It really will make a difference!

My dress is made from organic cotton.

My superhero outfit is made from cereal boxes.

NEXT STEPS

Look out for these **GOOD** materials when you shop:

- **linen**

- **organic cotton**

- **hemp**

- **Tencel** (look it up!)

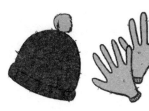

#21 ▶ TRY VEGAN!

We looked earlier at eating less meat and mainly eating veg and grains, but we also need to think about the amount of dairy and eggs we eat.

Going vegan means that you don't eat or use anything from an animal. No meat, no dairy (such as cow's milk). It also means avoiding some clothes or bathroom items too, if they contain animal products.

Now, this may not be something that you want to do completely, but even going vegan some of the time can have a positive effect on the planet – and give you some tasty new veggie meals!

Think about a plate of vegan food: fruits, vegetables and grains. To get that to your plate takes a lot less energy, land and water than a plate of non-vegan food. For a glass of milk, to look after the cows as they grow, to give them grain, to farm the land...it all takes ENERGY and makes a real dent in the natural world! In some parts of the world, people cut down trees to make new land to put the animals on – but those animals are only farmed to feed us. Doesn't sound like we're looking after God's garden particularly well...

Let's think too about animal welfare. That means treating our animals well. Some farmers really do and some farmers really don't.

To make milk, a dairy cow might be forced to have more baby calves than she should do. Sometimes, dairy cows are just seen as milk machines and are not looked after for what they are: creatures created by God the Creator!

What about eggs? Well, you only need female chickens – hens – to lay eggs, so male chicks aren't wanted. We're making the animal kingdom suit our needs. God's asked us to respect and look after all of it – not just to keep the bits we want, then throw away the rest!

DO YOUR BIT FOR CLIMATE CHANGE

- Eat less dairy and when you do, make sure you're supporting farmers who are looking after their animals.

- Try other milks – such as organic oat milk, European-grown organic soya milk, 'calf-friendly milk'.

- Can't resist your eggs? Buy organic or local.

- More veg. Less meat.

- Try new things!

My vegan meals to try:

....

....

....

VIRTUAL WATER

Eh?

How can water be virtual?

We drink water, we swim in water, we flush water (sorry, but it's true).

We also use water to make things – or factories do. In fact, the greatest amount of water we as a planet use...is to make the things we buy! That's what is meant when we talk about 'virtual water'.

We know that we need to use less water – we looked at that in an earlier chapter – but did you know...

- A large chocolate bar uses 1,700 litres in the production process. That's enough to fill 12 bathtubs!
- Foods such as avocados, mangoes and almonds all grow on very thirsty plants. Almonds are destroying the land they are grown on in California because of this.

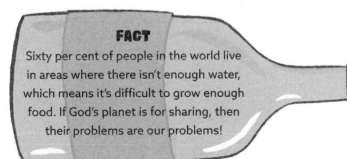

FACT
Sixty per cent of people in the world live in areas where there isn't enough water, which means it's difficult to grow enough food. If God's planet is for sharing, then their problems are our problems!

This means that the best ways to use less water are to buy fewer things and to eat food that uses less water to produce it, which is often grown locally.

Around the world, people keep moving to cities. Well, there are jobs there...but often there's not a lot of water there. In fact, many cities have water piped in. Also, look at the things we're buying. Things that use up a lot of water. You might be surprised...

THINKING OF THIRSTY THINGS

Just remember that things can be thirsty – not just humans! Beef, jeans, cotton, some fruits and nuts...Look at the 'water calculator' (at: <www.watercalculator.org/footprint/what-is-virtual-water>) to see how much water all these things use, even though we never see it! You could go through a list with your family and see what could be a treat instead of something that you buy all the time.

#23 BIBLE HUNT

The Bible is **FULL** of verses that teach us, guide us and tell us quite clearly that it's our job to **look after the planet!** So I guess we should do it, then.

Today's task?

- Find a Bible.

- Find a piece of paper and some coloured pens.

- Look up some of these Bible verses, and either write out the ones that make you think about protecting the planet or just your favourite words or sentences from the verses.

Psalm 24.1 This is a good one to start with: 'The earth is the Lord's and everything in it.'

Genesis 1.26...

Genesis 1.31...

Genesis 2.15...

Psalm 95.5...

Nehemiah 9.6...

Matthew 22.39...

John 1.3...

Ephesians 4.32..

Colossians 3.12...

Philippians 2.4..

You could draw a picture of the Earth or your favourite thing in nature – then write some of the words around it, in different colours.

Put your picture somewhere in your home that you'll see it. Maybe in your bedroom, on the fridge door or maybe in the window for neighbours to see?

Be inspired and reminded that this planet is God's, but we're the ones looking after it!

PROTEST!

Do you remember, in Chapter 3 we talked about writing to our MPs?

Done it yet?

Yes/No/All right, now I have

....

Did you hear back?

Yes/No/Well, I haven't written yet, so of course I haven't

....

There are other things that we can do to tell our government and businesses that we want them to change! If we want them to do things differently, to change what they believe and how they act (these are called 'policies') so that they can help nature and people living in poverty, then we need to let them know and **MAKE SOME NOISE!**

One way is to join a large group of people on the streets of cities in a big, organized event to shout about what we think should be done. You'd need to do this with your grown-ups and in a safe way! Find out if there's a climate march happening near you some time soon. You could join it and march and chant and wave signs and let the world know what you think!

Many peaceful protests have happened in history to make change happen. Here are some – you could look them up on Ecosia, or you might have heard about them in school:

- **William Wilberforce**
- **Martin Luther King Jr and the Civil Rights Movement**
- **Greta Thunberg**
- **the Tree Sitters of Pureora**
- **Jesus.**

Some of these were Christians, some children!

I'm painting my sign for the protest. I'm writing **BIG** – I want the world to see it!

At that size, I think the Moon could see it!

REAL-LIFE PLANET PROTECTOR!

Meet Niamh (9)

I first realized that we're causing huge problems to our climate when I saw it being talked about on *Blue Peter*. Then I saw that the UK Government has declared a climate emergency. I always thought that an emergency was…well, something you had to pay attention to right away, like **RIGHT NOW**, but they declared the emergency in April 2019 and it feels as though everyone is carrying on like before, like there is no emergency. It doesn't make any sense.

So I decided that, as well as making all sorts of changes to how we live as a family, I wanted to speak out about it and tell the Government to take action. So I've got involved with Extinction Rebellion Kids and have joined in with the school strikes that Greta Thunberg started. I've done campaigns, been in the paper, on the news and the radio. Sometimes it means that I get to have a few hours out of school, but mostly it means a lot of extra work on the weekends. Besides, I'd much rather be in school and not have to worry about climate change.

Why do I do it? Why do I give up my time to join protests, do research and make signs? Greta said, 'No one is too small to make a difference.' That means me…and it means you too. We are children, we can't undo what adults have done or what they do now, but it is **US** who will have to live with it. It will hurt and damage us, so it is **REALLY** important that we join in and we make our adults listen.

#25 LOOK UP

This is a fun activity that you can do any time you want some time out of your home. Coat on! (If it's cold or rainy.) As Planet Protectors it's important that we take time to appreciate nature.

If you have a garden, sit in it, or you can go to your local park or field or wherever the nearest nice green space is.

- What do you notice? What's the best thing you can see or hear?..

- Any animals?..

- How many birds or butterflies do you see?.....................

- Can you hear birdsong?...

- Let's look down for a moment. Can you see any insects?

  ....

Look up again. At the clouds. What are the different sorts you see? Can you draw one on the opposite page?

Walk somewhere different. Maybe under some trees or where you see other plants or animals.

What do you notice here? What do you see? Feel? Smell? Hear? Touch?

What has been your favourite thing that you've noticed?

....

Look up again. Thank God for all of this wonderful nature. Can you ask for God's help to protect it?

#26 BIRTHDAY LIST

Have you got a birthday this year? I have! I bet you do too.

What about Christmas? I bet you'll be celebrating that as well.

Now, what about presents? Do you ask for certain things or wait to see what someone buys you?

Lots of toys are made from plastic – and plastic isn't good for our planet.

If anyone asks you what you want for your birthday or Christmas, you **COULD** say to them, 'Nothing plastic please!' There are lots of brilliant, fun toys and games that don't contain plastic.

There are zero-waste pressies too. No packaging! What about experiences? Days out? Vouchers for fun activities?

FACT
Some experts say that, by 2050, the amount of plastic in the ocean will weigh more than the fish!

If you want to make a **BIIIIG** difference, you could always ask someone to make a donation to a charity – or even buy something for a family across the world, from mosquito nets to reading glasses to baby equipment.

My birthday list (ideally plastic-free!)

....

....

....

....

(Oh, and happy birthday. For when it's your birthday...)

Uncle Jon bought me this plastic toy. Should I feel bad?

Of course not! What's important now is that you **PLAY** with it and keep it for a long time instead of just binning it. Then, when you're finished with it, give it to a charity shop!

#27 ▶CHILDREN CHANGE CHURCHES, PART 2

Is your church an Eco Church?

What's an Eco Church? I hear you ask. (You can ask it out loud now if you want. You don't have to. The book can't hear you.)

An Eco Church is a church that's joined an awards scheme run by a charity called A Rocha UK. It shows that your church is serious about helping to protect this lovely creation.

Churches earn points by doing the right things to look after the planet. Those points earn a Bronze-, Silver- or Gold-level Eco Church award.

Send your church leader to <www.ecochurch.arocha.org.uk>. On that website, leaders can answer a few questions about things to do with your church.

- **Worship and teaching** Do your leaders make planet-saving sermons?
- **Buildings** Who supplies the electricity? What cups do you drink from?
- **Land** Is the land your church is on wildlife-friendly?
- **Community and global** Doing and helping ... Writing to your MP too (see page 17)!
- **Lifestyle** How we travel to church. What we throw away. What we eat ...

That could just mean sharing ideas from this book with your church! Plus your own BRILLIANT ideas too, of course. Speaking of which...

NEXT STEPS

What ideas can you think of to help in each of the five Eco Church areas?

Worship and teaching (What could get people talking?)

....

Buildings (Could your church change how they do anything?)

....

Land (Outside your church building – how could it attract more wildlife?)

....

Community and global (What ideas could you think of to get people doing good things locally?)

....

Lifestyle (How could your church change its habits for the better?)

....

Talk to your children's group leader. Could your group lead the way in helping to get the Eco Church award?

I don't think our church would get full marks for protecting God's planet.

Doesn't matter. **WE** wouldn't get full marks either! The point is: are we trying to *get better* at looking after the world?

28 ‹ BE A CLIMATE CHAMPION

OK. Time for a science lesson. Ready?

Here's the big issue. As a planet, we've used fossil fuels for years. They send out a gas called CO_2 (carbon dioxide), as well as other greenhouse gases. That means they act like a giant blanket or duvet around the world's atmosphere. What happens if you're under a duvet? You heat up.

The planet's heating up – and that's dangerous. It changes how the whole world works:

- **sea levels rise and icy glaciers melt**

- **species become extinct – their habitat changes and the food they rely on is only available at the wrong time**

- **coral reefs disappear**

- **extreme weather events happen much more often (the floods, droughts, storms, typhoons, hurricanes and forest fires we see on the news)**

- **food production goes down – for us, we might not be able to get bananas or chocolate(!), but for many, they won't get any food at all**

- **diseases spread and the poorest suffer most – how unfair!**

Imagine **LOTS** of sand on a beach ball. Lots of people like you and me, him and her, them and **ALL OF US** working together! That would be one sandy beach ball.

What can I do? I feel small compared with this huge planet. Like a speck of sand on a giant beach ball!

What if **EVERYONE** did one thing in each of these areas?

- **Personal** Choose one thing in your own life that will reduce your and your family's CO_2 emissions (you could look through other chapters if you need ideas).

- **Church** Get your church/children's group involved. Ask your leader to take a Sunday where you look at how Christians can respond to climate change.

- **Government** Ask the Government to stick to its promise to keep warming to below 1.5 °C and to stop supporting fossil fuel industries.

There are lots of ideas in this book to help you. The change starts with you...and you and you and you and her and him and them and **ALL OF US!**

REAL-LIFE PLANET PROTECTOR!

Meet Leo (7)

I went to the Sea Life Centre with my mum and dad when I was five, and saw how animals were dying from rubbish being thrown into the sea. They were getting stuck and eating it; other animals would then starve as they wouldn't get enough food. I'd also seen how sharks were being killed just for their fins and rhinos for their horns. This made me really upset and I knew that I had to do something about it.

I decided to raise money for turtles, to give to the groups that help them (they're my favourite), and adopt a lemur and a penguin, to look after them. I even helped to feed penguins at Peak Wildlife Park – it was so much fun! I did a beach clean and collected lots of rubbish from our local beach. While I was there, I made an awareness video for a charity called Shark Guardian, as well as for my school, to show how easy it is to take care of where we live.

I guess my biggest choice was my decision to become a vegetarian. I don't feel it is right to eat meat that has been processed. This is really damaging the environment and the animals are not leading good lives. I would love to see people change how they live: to stop polluting the seas, recycle as much as they can, help animals and end hunting. I love our planet and want others to enjoy it too.

#29 ▸ MONEY! PART 1

Do you get pocket money? Perhaps for doing a few jobs around the house? What do you do with that money? Maybe you save it up for something special . . . or spend it all in one go.

Do you give any of it away?

In the Bible, it says that God loves a cheerful giver!

I can be cheerful and I can be a giver! I just find it difficult to do both at the same time.

Jesus tells a story about a widow with not much money. She only put two small coins into the collection box, but Jesus says, 'She put in more than anyone else.' Others who were giving had lots of money – but what little she had, she gave gladly.

Giving when you don't have much is more valuable to God than giving when you have lots.

When I was a child, my dad talked with me about giving 10 per cent of my pocket money, and he said that if I got into the habit of giving away a regular amount when I didn't have

much, then I would find it easier to do when I was earning more. That has always stayed with me!

It doesn't have to be 10 per cent – the point is learning to give regularly and to think of others.

So what could you give to? What things do you care about most? Here are some ideas to start you off, but there are others too.

I want to help...	I could give to...
People living in poverty	Tearfund or Christian Aid or CAFOD
Fight climate change	Operation Noah, Tearfund, Christian Aid
Endangered animals	World Wildlife Fund or A Rocha

NEXT STEPS

Maybe save up together as a family and decide what to do with the money?

#3 ► MONEY! PART 2

Do you have a bank account yet? Maybe not. You may have an account somewhere with some savings in it. Perhaps your grown-ups will be thinking of setting up a bank account for you when you're older.

When you do get that bank account, you could get one that supports **ethical finance**.

What's ethical finance, then?

When you put money into a bank account, it's your money. The bank is just keeping it safe but, while it's there, they do something else with it. The bank **invests** the money – that means they use the money to help other companies do what they do.

So...what do these other companies do?

- **How much do each of these things matter to you? Mark each out of 10 or write why each is important.**

- **Some pollute the environment**...

- **Some don't look after animals**...

- **Some don't pay their workers properly**...........................

- **Some cut down forests**...

But there are many good companies too!

Triodos Bank is a good one, but there are others too. You should always research carefully with your grown-ups before putting your money **ANYWHERE**.

Ethical finance means having a bank account with a bank that invests our money in companies that are Planet Protectors, just like we are!

That's exciting – our money can help to look after the planet even when we're not spending it! We'll have to not spend money more often...

POND LIFE

Ponds are great ways to encourage wildlife. Lots of interesting, **DIFFERENT**, diverse, **MARVELLOUS** species of animals – frogs, newts, dragonflies, insects, birds (who like eating insects) – come to ponds to live, splash, soak or swim.

In the past 100 years, 70 per cent of ponds have vanished from the UK countryside, so every pond matters!

If you have a garden, you may not have room for a whole pond...but maybe you've got a corner where you could dig a hole and put a washing-up bowl in it? Maybe you have a birdbath or a trough? If you can fit one in, chat with your grown-ups about going big with a water feature!

I don't think that I can fit a pond into my garden.

That's fine. Let's visit some water in nature! A pond, a river, a lake... See what wildlife we can spot!

If you're up for the pond challenge, chat to your grown-ups and search online (for example, <https://rhs.org.uk>) for info about how to make a wildlife pond.

A POND FOR WILDLIFE

- For a **proper pond**, a long shallow slope will encourage wildlife to come and visit and help them to get in and out.
- For a **smaller container**, use pots or old barrels – but line them first to fill in any holes! Plug those leaks...
- Think about having **plants** in your pond – possibly floating ones.
- Lots of people think of ponds as having **fish**...but if you add fish, they'll probably eat lots of other wildlife that may come to play!
- **Be super-careful around ponds or water of any kind,** especially if you or your friends are young children! Make sure an adult is there to supervise.

Draw your perfect pond here. What's in it? Animals? Plants? Any funky waterfalls or fountains?

#32 ► HOME V. SCHOOL!

When it comes to protecting God's planet, does your school do things better than your home? Is it the other way round – your family is better than your class at being awesome about the world?

There may be some things your school could learn from your home...or your home from your school. Does your school recycle as much as you do at home? Who's better at dealing with food waste?

List here anything from this book that would be FAB for your school to do too.

Thing	Doing it at home?	Doing it at school?	Who wins?
Try vegan?	3 meals a week!	0 meals a week	Home!

...AND THE WINNER IS...HOME/SCHOOL (scribble out the loser)!

NEXT STEPS

- What can you do about it? Talk to your friends, teacher, headteacher?

- Could your school run an Eco Week to make us think about different topics? Could you give your teacher some ideas?

While you're thinking about school, how do you get there? Could you set an example to your friends by walking/cycling?

In this book, there are some ideas that could work for school as well as at home. We use a lot of bottles at our school and school leaves lights on all the time.

There's a great allotment at school, though. Some things they do really well! Everywhere's different.

#33 ENDANGERED SPECIES

Did you know, a quarter of all mammals are at risk of extinction? That is partly thanks to hunting, but also because of our human habits...habits which are damaging habitats!

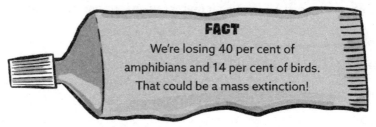

FACT
We're losing 40 per cent of amphibians and 14 per cent of birds. That could be a mass extinction!

Ugh. This is not a good fact. We need a good fact...

How about this then: did you know that Earth's history is divided into chunks of time called 'epochs'? For over 10,000 years, we've been in an epoch called the Holocene Epoch. Ooh, that's a good fact...

BUT some scientists say that, instead, we should call this the Anthropocene Era (*anthropos* is Greek for man or human), because we are living in a time when humans are changing the world so much – too much! Pulling down forests, building too many houses, changing the climate, overfishing, overfarming...

We're having a huge impact on other animals.

Oh dear. Another not-very-nice fact. Maybe by the end of the next page we'll have a good one...

NEXT STEPS

How about if we learnt to see other animals as God sees them. He made them and loves them. They're extremely precious to him.

- **List some endangered species here** (search with a grown-up on Ecosia if you're not sure).

- **Where in the world are they?**

- **What can we do to help them?** (Again, search online if you need help.)

What endangered animal?	Where is it?	What can we do?
Orangutan	Borneo	Use less palm oil!

Find out more from organizations such as the WWF and A Rocha, and check your piggy bank to see if you can help them out!

Here's a **GREAT** fact: doing many of the planet-protecting things in this book will help to protect animal species!

PALM OIL? FACEPALM...

#34

Sometimes, when it comes to endangered species, it's tricky to work out how we can help. We can't have orangutans home to live with us...can we? (No, no we can't. They'd wreck the spare room and imagine how much hair would get stuck in the bathroom plughole.)

But we are welcoming into our homes something that is the enemy of animals such as orangutans. There's a thing that's actually endangering endangered species...and we welcome this thing in nearly every time we come back from the shops! It's called palm oil.

You'll find palm oil in about half the packaged products in supermarkets! Pizza, chocolate, toothpaste, shampoo, ice-cream, crisps, bread...

LOADS of the rainforests in Malaysia and Indonesia have been burned down to free up land for palm oil plantations. Lots of animals were quite happy living there before...Between 1999 and 2015, the number of orangutans in Borneo **MORE THAN HALVED**. Since 1970, South and Central America have lost 89 per cent of their species!

NOT ONLY THAT, burning the rainforests releases lots of carbon dioxide into the atmosphere...which speeds up climate change.

We should stop using palm oil. Like, right now.

Well, yes, but... it's in everything! Well, not everything, but everything you had for lunch...

It is in **A LOT** of things! That doesn't mean we need to stop eating or using each of those things, but what we **CAN** do is:

Tick box when you've done it!

- **look at the label**

- **try to avoid products with palm oil in or at least reduce them**

- **buy products made with sustainable palm oil**

God made the world. When he looked at it he saw that it was good. Then humans came along and thought...we'd quite like to make a lot of biscuits with palm oil from that land. And the biscuits were tasty, but the orangutans needed somewhere to live. How will this story end? It's up to us!

NEXT STEPS

- Know your palm oil! Look out for it in what you buy.

- Chat to your grown-ups about the palm oil they use... probably without knowing it.

LIGHTS OUT!

We all do it.

We go into a room, turn the light on, leave the room...and forget to turn the light off.

If your grown-ups are moaning at you to '***Remember to turn your bedroom lights off!***' they're not just doing it to save money on their electricity bill.

All right, maybe they are – but there's a bigger reason to turn lights off and unplug phone chargers, computers, printers and other devices when we're not using them. It cuts energy use by an average of 20 per cent. That's 20 per cent *less* energy that the power stations need to provide! If those power stations burn fossil fuels (such as oil and gas), then we're actually harming our precious atmosphere by simply flicking a switch.

Dad says that I light up every room I walk into.

PUZZLE

Can you find which devices have been left on?

NEXT STEPS

Have a think about other power-saving planet-protecting opportunities around your home. Can you save electricity by:

- wearing more jumpers instead of reaching for the heating

- using natural light – sometimes the sun is all we need

- tracking your energy use with a Smart Meter

- unplugging appliances that you've not used in a while – does anyone NEED a waffle-maker plugged in ALL the time!?

FISH FINGERS FOR TEA!

Yum! Or should I say...Yum?

Now look, we're not here to ruin your fish finger fun, but next time you chomp down on one, think about where that fish has come from. Can you look at the packet?

If it has a nice logo on it – the Marine Stewardship Council (MSC) logo – it is a sign that the manufacturer is working to look after the fish stocks in the ocean when it catches fish for your fish fingers...

If you buy farmed fish, check it's RSPCA Freedom Food or organic. Try going to <www.mcsuk.org/goodfishguide/app> and download the Good Fish Guide from the Marine Conservation Society – it will help you to buy sustainable fish.

Why does this matter?

Well, our seas and oceans are important for life: the water cycle sustains life on the land; ocean currents send warmth around the world and they are a vital part of controlling how much CO_2 is in the atmosphere.

In our oceans, there are vast numbers of different marvellous God-breathed species, which he's put us in charge of! Humans need the oceans too – over 3 billion people rely on the seas and the coast for their jobs or as a source of food.

So it's important that we look after the seas and oceans – for people and the other creatures that depend on them. What do you think happens if we take **TOO MANY** fish and sea creatures out of the sea?

Why should we not take too many fish from the sea? Is it because the sea level would go down a bit, like when I take toys out of the bath?

No! It's that if we take too many, there won't be enough fish left.

The way we're taking them out is also causing massive damage. Bottom trawling is when huge nets are weighted down (sometimes with metal beams) and dragged across the sea floor. This type of fishing scoops up everything! Then the fish that are wanted (mostly cod and prawns) are taken and those not wanted are tossed back into the sea – except now they're no longer living. Imagine someone in the sky above your house dropping a huge net on your town and dragging it along till everything is destroyed. Bottom trawling is not nice for the sea floor.

The World Wildlife Fund says that more than 300,000 small whales, dolphins and porpoises die from entanglement in fishing nets each year. Does that sound as though humans are looking after the sea creatures like God asked us to?

Write your two-letter answer here..............

#37 ▶ STARGAZING

Look up. Up a bit more. Bit more still. There. Oh, and wait till it's night-time.

We've been looking down a lot in this book, at the planet at our feet, the world that's been home to humans for thousands of years. Let's now also look up and out, beyond this world into the incredible, dizzying space that is . . . well, space.

The world is one tiny object in a vast universe – so vast that we can hardly comprehend it. We're on one planet within a solar system . . . within a galaxy . . . within the universe.

Did you know, the Sun is one of between 200 billion and 400 billion stars in the Milky Way galaxy? Earth is just one of at least 100 billion planets? Our galaxy is just one of possibly two trillion galaxies!

Wow. Makes you think . . . Does it really matter if I don't tidy my room?

Pick a clear night, go outside, turn off **EVERY** light, lie on your back...and look up. What stars can you see? Can you spot any constellations?

Can you see the Moon? That Moon is 240,000 miles from the Earth – that's the average distance most of us will walk in our lifetime!

Imagine the Sun's the size of a peanut...then the Earth would be a grain of salt on that peanut. To represent the distance to the nearest star, another peanut would need to be taken 200 miles away.

That's just a trip round the corner compared to the furthest object seen in our universe: a small galaxy called GN-z11. It's so far away that when we see it (through the Hubble Space Telescope) the image we're seeing is that galaxy from 13.4 billion years ago. It's taken that long for the light to get back to us!

Isn't that amazing? God made all those things too!

DEAR SUPERMARKET...

Do you know how much power your local supermarket has? (And no, I don't just mean it sells batteries. Different sort of power.)

One third of all we spend goes to supermarkets. That means for every pound we spend on things, 30p of it is going to Tesco, Sainsbury's, Aldi, Lidl, Morrisons, Waitrose, Asda or whatever else you call the big building nearby that seems to sell **EVERYTHING**.

Some things that supermarkets sell could damage the environment. They only sell things that they think we want! Often the supermarkets think that we just like cheap things, even if they're bad for the planet.

So if we care about our planet, we need to **LET THE SUPERMARKETS KNOW!** Tell them that we don't just want cheap shopping – we want them to sell the **RIGHT** items. Supermarkets have the power do **SUPER THINGS** too!

If we tell them it matters more to us that they look after the planet and the people who provide the food they sell than keeping on lowering prices, then they'll think again. You're the customer, and don't they say that the customer is always right?

Let's write to our local supermarket and tell them what we want them to do!

Yes! But first I need to buy a pen and some paper. Better go to the supermarket, then.

FACT

Supermarkets in the UK create more than 800,000 tonnes of plastic packaging waste each year – that's the weight of 4,000 houses! The shops themselves are worth **180 BILLION POUNDS!** If they think you'll spend money with them, they'll listen.

NEXT STEPS

Contact your supermarket! Say what you think and what you want it to do.

You could email this letter to customer services via the supermarket's website, and/or arrange to hand it to the manager in the store. Here's an outline to get you started.

Dear Manager of *(name of supermarket)*

My name is.................................and I'm............years old. I shop at your supermarket. I think it's really important that *(look through this book – what do you think are the biggest issues about protecting the planet?)* ....

....

....

(What do you want the supermarket to do?)......................

....

....

(Include your address if you'd like a reply. Ask a grown-up's permission too!)

(Say goodbye nicely and sign your name. Practise signing your name here.)

....

THE PLASTIC-FREE BATHROOM

Do you want to have the **BEST BATHROOM** in the **WORLD?**

Well, now you can!

Surely the **BEST BATHROOM** in the **WORLD** would be a bathroom that doesn't *harm* the world?

It's going to be a challenge...because bathrooms are big plastic collectors!

> I've got too much plastic in my bathroom.

> Me too – and not just the Lego brick I found floating in the toilet.

Go into your bathroom. Have a look around and write down everything that is made of plastic. You've probably found a lot of things, but don't despair – it's easy to make the switch. You can now buy bamboo toothbrushes, shampoo bars, soap bars, refillable cleaning containers, wipes you can wash and use again rather than disposable ones...and so much else too. You just need to make the change!

The hopefully-not-big list of things made of plastic in your bathroom

Plastic		Non-plastic
....		....
....		....
....		....
....	Swap for	....
....		....
....		....
....		....
....		....

NEXT STEPS

- Start by choosing one thing to swap for the plastic version.

- Can you find non-plastic things instead to help you to protect the planet?

Done that? What's next to change, then? Toothpaste? Shampoo? Liquid hand wash?

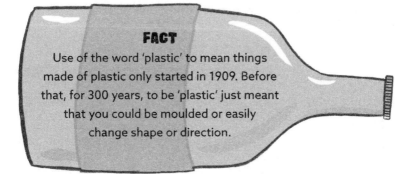

FACT

Use of the word 'plastic' to mean things made of plastic only started in 1909. Before that, for 300 years, to be 'plastic' just meant that you could be moulded or easily change shape or direction.

Can you change your plastic habit? How plastic-free can you be?

REAL-LIFE PLANET PROTECTORS!

Meet Mariella (11) and Kester (9)

We were sad and bored with picking up plastic litter from our local park and beach, so decided to help our mum with a plastic campaign in our city of Portsmouth. There's a fab organization called Surfers Against Sewage and they have a Plastic Free campaign where cities, towns and villages can work to become Plastic Free Communities, so we decided to join in and make Portsmouth a Plastic Free Community.

It involves getting businesses, schools and community groups to think about reducing their single-use plastic, and you also run litter picks and fundraisers. But the first thing that needed to happen was getting our local councillors to agree to the Council being involved.

We went to a full Council meeting and gave a short talk (they called it a 'deputation') about why we wanted our city to have less single-use plastic. We told them what we do at home and school, and explained the difference it would make to local wildlife. After our talk, the councillors had a vote to see if they would help and *all* 42 of them agreed with us. The councillors were very impressed that we were brave enough to talk in front of them all and we were the youngest people to do it in our city...so we also made history!

We've been doing lots of other things since and our city should be awarded Plastic Free status soon.

TECH A BREAK

We all love tech.

From video games to social media to TV and back to video games again, many children spend a **THIRD** of their awake time looking at screens!

That's an awful lot of time, so...why not take a break from screens?

REASONS TO TAKE A BREAK FROM YOUR TECH

- **Get outside!** It's nice out there. Even when the weather's not nice...nature's nice!

- **Your tech-break helps your brain.** Research shows that if we spend too long looking at screens, it can make us unhappy.

- **Power down.** Your devices use energy. A HUGE amount of energy is consumed by computers that are LEFT ON at night! Power down now and then. Let your tech go to sleep, let this planet heal...all by turning it off!

- **Are you online?** Be safe, don't put things online about YOU without a grown-up knowing, and ask yourself: is this still fun? If it stops being fun, stop. (Then do something fun.)

- **Laptops can use only a third of the energy a desktop computer does.** Got a desktop? Maybe change it to a laptop next time.

101

- **When you're ready to get rid of your device** – it's too slow, old or broken – **recycle it!** Then buy your next device second hand. It all helps to protect the planet.

To make those magical, lovely, **BRILLIANT** devices, from tablets to laptops to tabtops to laplets (just invented those – but someone will invent them soon), it takes some pretty special materials.

Ninety per cent of rare minerals come from China. Also, the Democratic Republic of Congo provides lots, but mining those materials has a big effect on the environment...and not a big enough effect on the wallets of the workers. They're not paid much to help make our computers and phones, and they work in awful conditions!

It all adds up to **BIG** emissions. In fact, by making and binning devices, the computing industry emits as much bad air into the world as the whole of the **PLANE** industry!

Technology's great – and it can be **GREAT** for the environment, if it helps to connect us so we stop travelling quite so much. Maybe your grown-ups travel less to work meetings, now they've worked out that they can have meetings online instead!

So use your tech for good! Connect with friends, find apps and websites that **HELP** our planet, not help to destroy it. Take a break now and then. Your computer goes to sleep when it's not being used. If your device can find time to take a break...why can't we?

#41 ▶ IT'S IN THE BOOK!

Have you got a Bible at home? Big book, isn't it?!

Many think of this as the story of God and humanity, but there's more to it than that. It's the story of God and **ALL** creation. Animals and plants and all of nature are included in the story that is in the Bible, and it says a lot about caring for the world.

Being a Christian means following what the Bible says. Here are a few things that you'll find in it...

- **There are 722 verses in the Bible that talk about water. It's seen as God-given and life-giving!**

- **God promises us land in the Old Testament. Handily, it's called the 'Promised Land'.**

- **In the book of Leviticus (25.1–2), God gives humanity lots of rules, including that we should give nature some time off now and then!**

- **There are LOTS of trees in the Bible. It starts with the Tree of Life and it ends with the Tree of Life!**

- **Jesus describes himself as a 'vine' and his followers as branches of that vine – like we're always growing, but rooted to Jesus.**

The Bible is **FULL** of trees, plants, animals, birds, sea creatures... Every beast from bees to beetles!

There's an ant in my Bible. It just crawled in.

The Bible may be a human story – but only because it's **US** who've messed things up. So we're the ones who need to put things right...and help to fix what we've done wrong to the planet!

Can you find some Bible verses telling us to look after the world? Try any of Deuteronomy 20.19, Psalm 96.11–12, Matthew 6.26 or Revelation 22.1.

Read the story of Noah – it's in the Bible, Genesis chapters 6—9, but you may have a children's version at home. The animals were protected by Noah and saved by God.

Draw the ark on the next page – don't forget to include your favourite animals!

MY ARK DRAWING

LOVE THE WATER WHERE YOU ARE

What water have you got near you? Pond? Lake? River? Canal?

Puddle. Of orange squash. I just spilled my drink.

Have you got water near you? Think about it for a moment. Maybe look at a map or think of any nearby walks that you've done.

The River Ganges is sacred to people of the Hindu religion. That means they think the world of it! They see it as closer to heaven than other places, and they send prayers by it. It's such a loved river that there are 108 different names for it! One of its names is *Nata-bhiti-hrt*, meaning 'Carrying away fear'. Another is *Sankha-dundubhi-nisvana*, meaning 'Making a noise like a conch-shell and drum'.

The people near the Ganges clearly think **A LOT** about their favourite river!

When you notice something, you look after it and you respect it. Next time you're near some open water, stop and look at it. Is it clean? Is there wildlife? Look closer – the creatures might be very small. Are there plants?

NAME YOUR WATER!

What name could you give your local pond or river? Is it 'Full of Plastic' or 'Duck Paradise'? I wonder if God's name for these watery areas would be different from our names for them.

Nickname for water near me: ....
....

Draw it here!

Nickname for other water near me: ....

....

Draw that here too!

Which one's your favourite? Why? What would make the other one nicer?

#43 TOILET TWINNING

Sixty per cent of people on the planet live in areas where there are problems to do with water: it's either too dirty or there isn't enough (or both). One of these people is Ungwa and she lives with her three children in the Democratic Republic of Congo. Here it is on a map of Africa.

DEMOCRATIC REPUBLIC OF CONGO

'I would have to leave home at four or five in the morning to fetch water to drink,' she says. 'And we had a serious problem with sicknesses like diarrhoea, typhoid and fevers.'

Lots of people like Ungwa (often mums and children) walk miles to collect their water, meaning that the children can't get their school work done and their mums have less time to do other things (such as growing food or working to bring in money).

As for toilets…they're a luxury! Many people don't have access to a decent working loo. Ungwa's village had a very dirty toilet, so people would do what they needed to do in the bush surrounding the village. People got sick easily and it wasn't safe.

There is a solution. Just like those bins earlier, you can 'twin' your toilet! You donate money and, in return, get a certificate to hang in your toilet, complete with a photo of the toilet *you* have helped! It might look different from yours, but it'll be a cleaner, nicer toilet, with cleaner, nicer water, all thanks to you. Head to <www.toilettwinning.org> to learn more.

Oh, and Ungwa? Her village now has clean, safe water, thanks to Tearfund, the charity behind Toilet Twinning (it's just started Tap Twinning too!). Ungwa's toilet still looks different from your toilet, but it's got 'tippy-tap' handwashing, a pit to get rid of horrid rubbish…and now the water's improved, her family is much healthier!

Could you write a prayer for Ungwa and those like her?

....

....

....

....

....

44

PSST! PASS IT ON

Who doesn't love a new toy or new item of clothing? Not us!

Because we're **Planet Protectors**, so we know (or we're learning) that, actually, new isn't always best. The simple fact is that we are consuming far too much.

'Consumption' means the number of things we buy, which are made from materials, which come from the ground, which use up energy, which has a lasting effect on the planet. If we slow down our consumption and buy less, use less, we don't have such a bad effect on God's world.

Ever had a yard sale? You might call it a garage sale, a jumble sale, a car boot sale . . . or you could not sell anything – you could give it away. School uniform, toys, games, shoes, coats . . . there are **LOADS** of things that we can pass on to other people.

Recently, we had a **BIG** clear-out and filled boxes and boxes with clothes and toys that we'd outgrown. We put those boxes at the end of our drive with a sign saying 'Help yourself!' It was great to see local people pass by, stop, look, pick something up, smile, take it home and get new use out of our things. (Yes, we were secretly spying from the window!)

There are Facebook and other online groups offering things that people are ready to pass on. Children outgrow clothes **FAST** and those clothes can be **LOVED** by other people!

You also save money and with that money you could do some good!

Maybe you're not ready to move on some items yet... but look around at your clothes, toys, games and books.

When you've finished with them, which friends could you offer them to?

You could also give them locally to others you don't know.

Thing	Who might like it?	If that person doesn't want it...?
Spotty shirt	My friend Danny	Charity shop
....	....	....
....	....	....
....	....	....
....	....	....

45

ONE, TWO, TREE

Trees are great. Where would we be without trees? Well, we wouldn't be here. Trees produce oxygen, which we breathe. They also absorb carbon dioxide, so that's very kind of them too. Good old trees.

Did you know, there are over **3 TRILLION** trees on Planet Earth. A third of our planet is covered in them! But that's way less than it used to be and we're causing terrible problems to the planet by cutting down so many of them.

The Bible starts with a tree and ends with a tree – and there are lots of trees in the middle too!

The oldest trees in the world are around 4,000 years old! That means there are trees still alive and growing today that were already over 1,000 years old *when Jesus was born!*

Mind. Blown.

Appreciate your trees! That includes the branches they grow, the ground they're in, the roots you may or may not be able to see. What about the soil we grow our crops and other plants in? It's all really quite amazing.

HELP YOUR TREES!

Buy recycled toilet paper, kitchen roll and other paper. Think creatively about wrapping paper, which often can't be recycled.

If you buy something wooden, look for the Forest Stewardship Council (FSC) logo or ask where the wood comes from. Using FSC-certified wood won't harm the world's forests.

It's worth making such small changes when we shop to take care of our plants, our soil... and our mighty, **BRILLIANT**, often incredibly *ooooooold* trees.

46

FEED THE BIRDS

You want to welcome wildlife to your garden, right? (Because, really, it's God's garden and God's wildlife.)

You want to do that in an eco-friendly way, right? (Because we don't want to harm the natural world when we make things.)

Then this is the page for you!

Now, you **COULD** make a bird feeder… but lots of them use old bottles or tins. It's not so nice to mix artificial materials with nature. Plus, we're SURE you don't have any old single-use plastic bottles in your home… right?! What a good Planet Protector you are!

Instead, here's how to *MAKE YOUR OWN FAT BALLS*, to bring birds to your place.

INGREDIENTS

- Vegetable oil or lard or beef suet
- Bird seed mix
- Some string

1 Put 1 part oil/lard/suet with 2 parts bird seed into a saucepan and warm it. Gently stir until the fat has melted.

2 Using an ice-cream scoop or spoon (because it will be hot), mould the mixture into as many balls as you want. Do get an adult to help.

3   Using a thin stick or a pencil, make holes through the fat balls. Thread the string through.

4   Separate them out on a tray and, once cool, pop them in the freezer, making sure that they're not touching.

5   Once they're frozen, you can take them out to your garden and find the best places to hang them.

Looks good enough to eat . . .

I wouldn't! Leave it for the birds.

Bon appetit, birdies!

#47 ▶ CRAFTY CLUBS

Do you do any clubs? After-school ones or on the weekends? You might go to a sports club or Beavers, Cubs, Brownies, Boys' Brigade, Girls' Brigade, art club, craft club...

There are things your clubs and groups can do to help look after the planet – just like at home and at school.

Three things to think about

1 **Travel** How do you get to your club? Walking, cycling, public transport, driving? The first three options are great for the planet, of course!

2 **Things** If there are arts and crafts involved, does your club use glitter or shiny paper? Most of these can't be recycled and leftover bits are often thrown away. Could they instead be *JUST AS CREATIVE* with natural products? If you're doing crafts, think about stones, flowers, fir cones, feathers... What could your club use for its activities that don't cost the Earth?

3 **Topics** Some clubs have badges or awards to work towards, or themed sessions. Maybe one topic could be protecting the planet? Chat to your leaders about featuring some environmental activities. What can you do as a group to help the issues that matter most to you? Could you:

- clean up the park

- learn more about climate change

- help protect animals?

List your other favourite Planet Protecting ideas here:

....

....

....

....

....

Then take them to your leader!

I was a Beaver and now I'm a Cub. They're both named after animals!

In my dance class, we're learning how to move like animals. It helps me to think more about God's brilliant creation.

PETS

'The godly care for their animals'.

That's what the Bible says in Proverbs 12.10. Good, righteous people look after the animals they're in charge of.

For many of us, that means pets! Do you have a cat or a dog, a hamster or a goldfish? How much caring do you do for your pets? Apart from stroking them now and then (well, I'm not sure anyone strokes goldfish). Do you walk them, comb them if they need it (again – not goldfish), make sure they're clean and healthy? Is your pet just an animal that lives with you or do you play an active part in looking after it?

> I don't have any pets... but I can still make sure that I look after the animals I meet.

> Yes! Whether it's my dog or a bird in your garden or the worm that lives outside your bedroom window...

The Bible starts with a story of God putting the first man and woman into the Garden of Eden. He tells us to look after the animals... It's like we're still there! Just as God looks after us, we should look after the animals he's given us.

Remember too that some animals might be best living in their natural habitats. Not every animal should be a pet. Also, if you're buying a pet, make sure that your grown-up knows to get one from the right place. There are responsible, good ways to get a pet (giving a rescue cat a new home maybe) and there are not-so-good ways to get a pet (avoid puppy farms!).

Oh, and take care with pet food too! Avoid pet food that's got factory-farmed ingredients in it, has been tested on animals or contains palm oil. Pets can eat ethically, just like us!

DRAW YOUR PERFECT PET!

Then, around it, what other things do you need to look after it?

Food? Collar? Clean water? Bed/aquarium/pond?

Hope you've not got much junk in your home!

If you do have some, though, before you put it in the recycling bin, could you turn it into something?

Why buy a plastic castle . . . when you can make one out of a cereal packet?!

Why buy a toy theatre . . . when you can make one out of a shoe box?!

Why buy a bowling set . . . when you can make bowling pins out of kitchen roll middle-bits and a ball from rubber bands?!

Toilet roll cardboard tubes or milk cartons . . . our next toys and games could be sitting in the fridge or cupboard, waiting to be turned into something . . .

. . . but they're a bit busy right now holding drink and loo paper!

Of course – if you can – limit the junk at home anyway. Cereal packets may be a thing of the past if you refill with a container. We get waaaaaaay too much packaging in the post when parcels are delivered, but hopefully companies will improve this in the future.

So maybe our homes will get less junk-filled? We hope so!

As Planet Protectors, make your junk modelling as eco-friendly as possible:

- **if you're decorating your junk model, think of natural materials: stones and flowers, maybe, rather than glitter and stickers (which you can't recycle)**

- **use pens to colour in, if you need to, rather than paint**

- **when you've finished your junk model masterpiece, enjoy it…but make sure you can recycle it as easily as when it was a cereal box or toilet roll tube (it's pretty tricky to recycle something that you've covered with sticky tape and glitter and paint and topped off with a plastic unicorn!)**

Hmm…what will you turn into what?

Get junk modelling – have fun!

On this page, we're **NOT** going to tell you to turn your screens off. We're **NOT** going to tell you to put down your tablet or computer and go play outside. We're going to say...

KEEP IT ON!

...but spend some time on it thinking about the planet.

There are **LOTS** of apps and games that can help us to appreciate the planet better.

Maybe you play Minecraft, Blockcraft, Planetcraft, Sim City or any of the other world-building games out there. Think about what you build – from houses to cities – and how that fits alongside nature. Some games show you the actual effects of big-city building on the natural world. In Sim City, you can design a city using sustainable energy options: solar, wind farms, geothermal...and you can see the effect of pollution if your city gets too big. In Minecraft, you can choose to create an eco-friendly world of no pollution...or you can create hazards! What will you choose?

Lots of video game designers have started 'Playing for the Planet' – games such as Angry Birds 2, Subway Surfers and Golf Clash now include mini-games and messages about caring for the environment.

You can also learn, read and expand your mind. Sit down with a grown-up and have all your questions answered at <www.dkfindout.com> – it's a great online encyclopaedia especially for children, with loads of articles about science, nature and **EVERYTHING!**

I always ask my parents before looking at anything online.

Me too. I mean, I ask my parents. I don't ask yours.

If you're watching TV as a family, how about a great wildlife show? There are some for children, like Steve Backshall's TV shows, and some for grown-ups too, like David Attenborough's *Planet Earth* or *Blue Planet*. Look out for *Springwatch* and *Autumnwatch*, with live programmes telling you what nature you can see **RIGHT NOW** in your garden!

What sort of TV show would YOU make about the planet?

What's your show's title?

....

Who'd host it? Maybe you or someone you like on TV?

....

Which part of the world would it be set in?

....

Does it feature animals or plants?

....

What message do you want viewers to take away with them?

....

....

....

5 ▶ PICK YOUR OWN!

From garden centres to farms, pick-your-own fruit and veg is a great way to, er, well...pick your own fruit and veg! In the Bible, Ecclesiastes 3 says, 'For everything there is a season', and there is! In fact, if you visit a pick-your-own place, you'll see different fruit and veg there at different times of the year.

You can see where your food comes from and be part of its journey from plot to plate...from mud to mouth...from ground to gulp...

You pick, you weigh, you pay, you go home, you eat. Yum!

We can pick asparagus in May, strawberries in June, raspberries and potatoes in the summer, apples and tomatoes in September and October, cabbages in November...

I love pumpkins in the autumn – and then a Christmas tree in December! Not to eat, though.

Genesis 8.22 says, 'As long as the earth remains, there will be planting and harvest, cold and heat, summer and winter, day and night.' God made these happen – and we can see them and feel them and touch them, and realize it's all part of the food that we eat. Sure enough, as the year goes on, the weather changes and different food grows, so no two trips to pick-your-own places will mean that you bring back the same goodies!

WHATCHA PICKING?

...and howdya find it?

	Describe it	**Name it**
What was the prickliest to pick?		
Heaviest fruit/veg?		
What wasn't ready yet?		
Priciest pick?		
Brightest colours?		
What was there most of?		
Looked yummiest!		

Can you draw these vegetables on the next page?

Now eat them!

52 NOW SHOUT ABOUT IT!

Now you've read this book (or at least reached the last page, even if you've not read **ALL** of it), what's next?

Well, tell. Yell! Make sure that you let people know what you think about the importance of protecting God's planet.

You could tell your friends. Share with three friends your favourite page from this book. Is there one activity that you think they'd enjoy doing too?

Is there one cause or idea that you think about a lot? It could be protecting wildlife, stopping climate change, using less energy, saving water...or any of the other areas we've looked at.

If you care lots about that idea, you'll be able to tell your friends about it. Maybe they might be inspired too?!

What then?

Well, could those three friends tell three *more* friends...and if they tell three more friends, then that would give you **40 PEOPLE** now knowing how good it is to be a Planet Protector!

Even if you tell just one person, you're still making a difference. What if you told your school? Your teacher? Your vicar?

Keep talking about protecting God's planet. Write stories about nature. Draw pictures of animals in their habitats. The more you talk, write, draw and tell the story of what we need to do, the bigger the difference you'll make in the world.

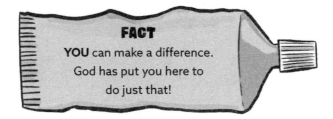

FACT
YOU can make a difference.
God has put you here to
do just that!

REFERENCES

A lot of the material in this book is drawn from Ruth Valerio's
L is for Lifestyle (revised edition, IVP, 2019) or her **Saying Yes
to Life** (SPCK, 2019) or the following sources.

5 Beachcombing
<www.sas.org.uk/our-work/plastic-pollution/plastic-
pollution-facts-figures>

6 The Big Sort
<www.mckinsey.com/business-functions/sustainability/
our-insights/style-thats-sustainable-a-new-fast-fashion-
formula>

10 Welcome!
<www.unhcr.org/uk/media-centre.html>

11 No throw
<https://wrap.org.uk/sites/default/files/2020-11/Food-
surplus-and-waste-in-the-UK-key-facts-Jan-2020.pdf>

22 Virtual water
<www.wateraid.org/au/articles/wateraid-report-reveals-
nations-with-lowest-access-to-water>

26 Birthday list
<www.ellenmacarthurfoundation.org/publications/the-
new-plastics-economy-rethinking-the-future-of-plastics-
catalysing-action>

31 Pond life

<www.devon.gov.uk/environment/wildlife/habitats-and-species/ponds-and-wetlands>

45 One, two, tree

<www.scienceinschool.org/content/world-without-trees>

<http://rmtrr.org/oldlist.htm>